Rescue Boats

by Valerie Bodden

CREATIVE
PAPER BACKS

RESCUE
VEHICLES

Published by **Creative Paperbacks**
P.O. Box 227, Mankato, Minnesota 56002
Creative Paperbacks is an imprint of The Creative Company
www.thecreativecompany.us

Design and production by **Rob & Damia Design**
Art direction by **Rita Marshall**
Printed by Corporate Graphics in the United States of America

Photographs by **Alamy** (19th era, Paul Bock, Guy Harrop, North Wind
Picture Archives), **Corbis** (Rick Friedman, Bob Sacha), **Dreamstime**
(Fibobjects, Thomas Perkins, Stocksnapper, Ling Xia), **iStockphoto**
(Nikki Bidgood, Alena Dvorakova, Oleksandr Kalinichenko, Paul Laliberte,
Manuel Salazar Peris, Linda Steward, Mark Wragg)

The Library of Congress has cataloged the hardcover edition as follows:

Bodden, Valerie.
Rescue boats / by Valerie Bodden.
p. cm. — (Rescue vehicles)
Summary: A fundamental introduction to water-based rescue vehicles
known as rescue boats, including their history, a description of their features,
and how they help people in emergencies.
Includes bibliographical references and index.
ISBN 978-1-60818-007-3 (hardcover)
ISBN 978-0-89812-578-8 (pbk)
1. Search and rescue boats—Juvenile literature. I. Title. II. Series.

VM466.S4B63 2011
363.12'381—dc22   2009048829
CPSIA: 012411 PO1420

9 8 7 6 5 4 3 2

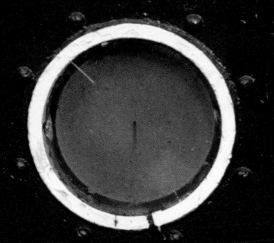

Contents

Sometimes people need help. They might be hurt. Or they might be lost. When people need to be saved at sea, a rescue boat might come to help them.

Rescue boats can get people out of unsafe places

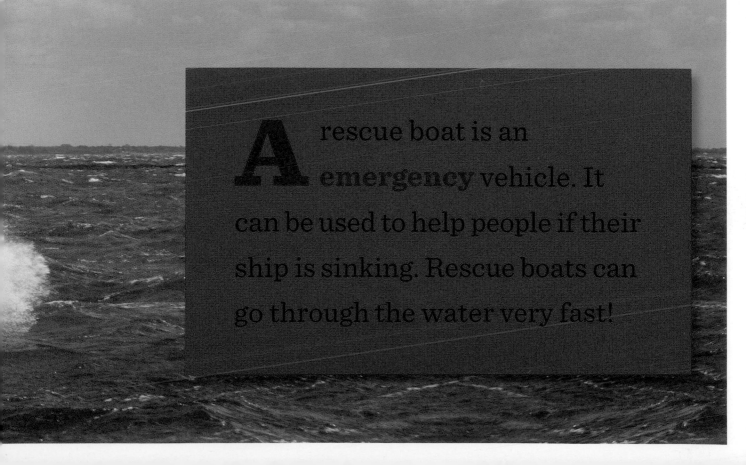

A rescue boat is an emergency vehicle. It can be used to help people if their ship is sinking. Rescue boats can go through the water very fast!

The first rescue boat was built about 200 years ago. People had to use **oars** or sails to make early rescue boats move. About 100 years ago, people started building rescue boats with **motors**.

Some rescue boats are made to rescue people close to shore. These boats are small and have flat bottoms. Bigger boats are used to rescue people who need help in deeper waters.

Covered areas with windows keep rescue workers safe and dry, too

Many rescue boats have sirens (*SY-runs*) and flashing lights. They carry ropes, life jackets, and **first-aid** supplies. Most rescue boats have parts called buoyancy (*BOY-un-see*) tanks. The tanks are filled with air. They flip the boat back up if it tips over in the water.

If people on a ship need to be rescued, they call for help over the radio. The workers on a rescue boat rush into action! One person drives the boat. He or she is called the coxswain (*KOK-sun*).

Rescue workers near shore can often see trouble before a dispatcher calls

When a ship is stuck out at sea, the rescue workers might throw it a rope. The rescue boat may pull it to shore. If a ship is sinking, the rescue workers help people get off. Then they help the people onto the rescue boat.

Sometimes the workers on a rescue boat have to get into the water. They rescue people who have fallen off a boat. Divers might look for people who have gone under the water.

Rescue workers practice saving people who have fallen into the water

The rescue boat brings everyone safely to shore. Then the boat is taken back to its **base**. The workers clean it and check its supplies. They make sure it is ready for the next emergency!

Long ago, people often had to use their own boats to rescue others

Early Rescue Boats

Long ago, fishing boats were used to rescue people at sea. Then special boats made just for rescuing people were built. They had to be rowed or sailed. In the 1700s and 1800s, buoyancy tanks were added to rescue boats so that they could go through bad storms without sinking.

Glossary

base

the place where an emergency vehicle is kept
when it is not being used

emergency

something bad that happens suddenly, such
as a car accident or fire

first-aid

having to do with the help given to someone who
is sick or hurt before the person gets to a hospital

motors

machines that make things, such as cars, move

oars

long poles that are flat on one end
and are pushed through the water
to move a boat forward

Read More

Ethan, Eric. *Rescue Boats.* Milwaukee: Gareth Stevens Publishing, 2002.

Lindeen, Carol. *Rescue Boats.* Mankato, Minn.: Capstone Press, 2005.

Web Sites

Canadian Coast Guard: What Belongs on Your Boat?

http://www.ccg-gcc.gc.ca/eng/Kids/Boat

Play a game about boating safety.

United States Coast Guard Coloring Books

http://www.uscg.mil/top/downloads/coloring.asp

Learn how rescue boats are used to help people.

Index